MANGO DIP

4 TABLESPOONS MANGO CHUTNEY

2 TEASPOONS DIJON MUSTARD

CURRY POWDER

8oz PHILLY CHEESE.

·TESCO· COOKERY· COLLECTION·

COOKING FOR TWO

TESCO

Published exclusively for Tesco Stores Ltd,
Delamare Road, Cheshunt, Herts, EN8 9SL
by Cathay Books, 59 Grosvenor Street, London W1

First published 1985

© Cathay Books 1985

ISBN 0 86178 310 7

Printed in Hong Kong

ACKNOWLEDGEMENTS

Series Art Director Pedro Pra-Lopez
Editor Nicole Foster
Photographer James Jackson with *stylist* Alison Williams
Food prepared for photography by Michelle Thomson

CONTENTS

NOTE

Standard spoon measurements are used in all recipes

1 tablespoon (tbls) = one 15 ml spoon
1 teaspoon (tsp) = one 5 ml spoon
All spoon measures are level

All eggs are sizes 3 or 4 (standard) unless otherwise stated.

For all recipes, quantities are given in both
metric and imperial measures. Follow either set
but not a mixture of both, as they are not interchangeable.

We set up our Consumer Advisory Service in response to the many pleas for information and cooking ideas we received from our customers. It is run by our team of qualified home economists who answer queries, offer practical advice on cookery and the home and give talks and demonstrations on new products and equipment.
The resounding success of the service and the continued demand for more and more recipes and information has now prompted us to produce our own special range of Tesco Cookery Books.
Our series starts with 12 books, each one focusing on an area that our customers have shown particular interest in. Each book contains practical background information on the chosen subject and concentrates on a wide selection of carefully tested recipes, each one illustrated in colour.

Cooking for Two offers some refreshing new ideas to those people who don't have to worry about cooking for the kids. Single people and couples of all ages and lifestyles enjoy the pleasures of creative cooking and the recipes in this book reflect that, whilst taking into consideration time and cost. These are suggestions for cosy suppers, quick snacks and three-course special occasion menus together with tips and hints on how to make effective use of the food and money available.
I've used many of these recipes at home and found them very successful. I hope you will enjoy looking through the book and trying some of the dishes for yourselves. Happy Cooking!

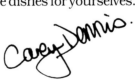

Carey Dennis, senior home economist, Tesco Stores Ltd.

INTRODUCTION

Most of us 'cook for two' at one time or another in our lives – whether as single people inviting a friend to a meal, young-marrieds rushing in from work, mothers with young children at home, or couples enjoying the comparative leisure of retirement. Such a wide variety of situations calls for a wide selection of dishes and menu suggestions – which we have tried to meet in this book.

Economy for two
It can be tempting when cooking for two to spend a lot of money on the more expensive, quick-cooking cuts of meat, such as steaks and chops, overlooking the more economical choices. Cheaper cuts of meat do require longer cooking in a conventional oven, and so one tends to think of casseroles, for example, as only being economical for 4 or more servings. But, a casserole for 4 can serve 2 people on two separate occasions, and small quantities of less expensive meat can be successfully cooked in a slow cooker or pressure cooker. Offal, especially liver and kidneys (see Liver with sage, page 26, Kidneys stroganoff, page 40), makes a reasonably priced meal for two, and has the extra advantage of cooking quickly. Fish – also quick-cooking – can provide handy servings for two (two plaice or a large lemon sole will divide conveniently into four fillets) and fish steaks (see page 19) or kebabs (see page 18) are perfect for two people.

Pasta also makes a lot of sense for two people: try spaghetti or tagliatelle with a variety of sauces such as tuna (see page 25), or buy fresh ravioli or tortelloni, available from delicatessen counters, and serve with a home-made tomato sauce.

Cooking for two can be specially enjoyable because it provides a greater opportunity for experiment than most family meals. It is much easier to attempt dishes which have to be served immediately, such as soufflés, when there's only one person to call to the table, and catering for two will undoubtedly encourage you to try your hand at brand-new recipes.

Planning the meal
A meal for two certainly does not have to be a hurried one-course affair. The *soups and starters* section gives a wide range of interesting first courses, none of which takes very long to prepare. Many of these starters can double up as a main dish for an informal light lunch or supper.

When there are two of you, and time is at a premium, it is tempting to open a few cans or run to the nearest 'takeaway'. And there are easy ways of presenting such food temptingly: canned crab bisque, for instance, can be transformed by the addition of a few tablespoons of sherry; taramasalata bought from a delicatessen counter and served in a halved avocado makes a really special starter, for example; and when you are only shopping for two, you may feel you can justify buying a portion of really luxurious pâté. However, our *quick and easy* dishes section provides a selection of recipes which are nutritious, more economical – and really just as quick. A freezer can also be a particularly useful standby when catering for two as you can store away cooked meals in 2-portion packs, and just reheat them when you want to eat.

Solutions for variety
The *main dishes* section again emphasizes variety, not only in what you cook but the way you cook it. Frying and grilling are probably the most frequently used cooking methods when cater-

ing for two but our suggestions also include suitable casseroles and roasts: a joint of meat for two makes good sense if the leftovers can be used in another dish the next day, like Lamb fricassee (see page 37), or the meat left over from a roast chicken can be made into a really appetizing salad if combined with freshly cooked rice, sweet peppers and mushrooms, and then tossed in mayonnaise. Or make an exotic salad combining leftover chicken strips with avocado mango or pineapple.

Fruit and cheese make a perfect end to any meal, whether for ten or two, but there are always occasions when a pudding really does add the finishing touch. The *desserts* section offers a variety of hot and cold sweets and puddings to round off your meal.

Finally, we give you three *special occasion menus* for celebratory dinners. Each dish is fairly simple and quick to prepare, the menus are well balanced, and planned to look attractive as well as taste delicious.

Suggested menu selections

For everyday meals, here are some suggestions for a week's evening meal menus, all using recipes in this book:

MONDAY

Prawn and cream cheese pâté (p.15)
Eggs Greek-style (p.26)
Apple crisps (p.47)

TUESDAY

Chilled avocado soup (p.7)
Mackerel with lemon and orange stuffing (p.30)
Oaty apricot crumble (p.52)

WEDNESDAY

Mushrooms à la grecque (p.13)
Normandy chicken (p.40)
Lemon mousse (p.50)

THURSDAY

Fresh tomato soup (p.8)
Beef stifado (p.32)
Atholl Brose (p.50)

FRIDAY

Eggs Mimosa (p.16)
Kidneys stroganoff (p.40)
Pears in white wine (p.54)

SATURDAY

Minted melon and orange cocktail (p.111)
French roast leg of lamb (p.36)
Cassata cheese (p.47)

SUNDAY

Tomato and mozzarella salad (p.14)
Lamb fricassee (p.37)
Rhubarb fool (p.53)

SOUPS AND STARTERS

Chilled avocado soup

1 large ripe avocado
1 tsp lemon juice
1 celery stalk, finely chopped
1½ tsp tomato purée
2 × 150 g (5·29 oz) cartons natural
  yoghurt
about 150 ml (¼ pint) cold chicken
  stock, skimmed of fat if homemade
dash of Tabasco sauce
salt and pepper
1 tbls snipped fresh chives, to garnish

Halve the avocado, remove the stone and scoop out the flesh into a large bowl. Add the lemon juice and mash the avocado with a fork until very smooth and creamy or purée in a blender.

Stir in the remaining ingredients, adding enough chicken stock to give a pouring consistency. Season to taste with salt and pepper.

Cover the bowl and stand it in a bowl of ice cubes. Chill in the refrigerator for 30 minutes. (Do not leave in the refrigerator for more than 1 hour or the avocado will discolour.) Garnish the soup with snipped chives and serve in chilled individual soup bowls.

Serving ideas: Serve for a summer lunch with French bread. Garnish each bowl with an ice cube if liked.
Variation: Use ¼ cucumber, peeled and grated, instead of the celery.

• Chilled avocado soup

Fresh tomato soup

15 g (½oz) margarine or butter
1 small onion, chopped
½ carrot, chopped
1 small celery stalk, chopped
225 g (8 oz) ripe tomatoes
300 ml (½ pint) chicken stock
2 tsp tomato purée
pinch of sugar
pinch of dried marjoram
salt and pepper
2 tbls soured cream, to finish

Melt the margarine in a large saucepan, add the onion, carrot and celery and fry gently for 5 minutes until softened. Add all the remaining ingredients, season to taste and bring to the boil. Cover the pan and simmer for about 20 minutes or until the carrot is soft. Remove from the heat and set aside to cool slightly.

Place the mixture in a blender goblet and process until smooth. Pass the mixture through a fine sieve into the rinsed out saucepan.

Reheat and adjust the seasoning to taste. Serve the soup in heated individual soup bowls, each serving topped with 1 tbls soured cream.

Serving idea: Serve with warm wholemeal rolls.
Variation: Add 1 tbls cooked rice to the soup just before serving.

● Fresh tomato soup
Chicken and sweetcorn soup

Chicken and sweetcorn soup

25 g (1 oz) margarine or butter
1 onion, finely chopped
1 large potato, diced
15 g (½ oz) plain flour
300 ml (½ pint) hot chicken stock
198 g (7 oz) can creamed sweetcorn
salt and pepper
50-100 g (2-4 oz) cooked boneless
  chicken, skinned and diced
2 tsp chopped fresh parsley, to garnish

Melt the margarine in a large saucepan, add the onion and potato, cover and cook very gently for 10-15 minutes, stirring from time to time, until the vegetables are soft but not coloured.

Stir in the flour, cook for 1 minute, then gradually stir in the chicken stock. Add the sweetcorn and simmer gently for 15-20 minutes until the potato is tender.

Pass through a sieve or liquidize and return to the rinsed out pan. Season to taste and stir in the chicken. Reheat gently and serve in heated individual soup bowls, garnished with a little chopped parsley.

Serving idea: Serve the soup with chunks of hot wholemeal or crusty French bread.

Variations: For crab and sweetcorn soup use a small can of crabmeat instead of the chicken. A finely chopped small red or green pepper may be added with the sweetcorn. Use two large spring onions instead of the onion.

Mixed fish soup

1 tbls vegetable oil
1 small onion, chopped
1 celery stalk, chopped
198 g (7 oz) can tomatoes
1 garlic clove, crushed
pinch of dried thyme
2 parsley sprigs
salt and pepper
225 g (8 oz) whiting fillet, skinned and
  cut into large pieces
1 small mackerel, filleted, skinned
  and cut into large pieces
10 peeled prawns or cooked, shelled
  mussels

Heat the oil in a saucepan, add the onion and celery and fry gently for 5 minutes until softened. Add the tomatoes with their juice, and the garlic and herbs. Season to taste with salt and plenty of pepper and stir well to mix.

Carefully place the whiting and mackerel pieces in a single layer over the vegetables and pour over enough water to just cover. Bring to the boil, then reduce the heat and simmer for 8 minutes. Add the prawns and simmer for a further 5 minutes until the fish is tender when tested with a fork. Serve the soup immediately, in heated individual soup bowls.

Serving idea: Serve with hot garlic or herb bread.
Variations: Any firm white fish may be used instead of whiting, and red mullet may replace the mackerel. Vary the fish according to availability and price – the total weight should be about 450 g (1 lb). Add a pinch of powdered saffron with the fish, if liked, to give the soup extra colour. Garnish the soup with chopped fresh thyme or parsley, or celery leaves.

• Mixed fish soup; Minted melon and orange cocktail

Minted melon and orange cocktail

½ small, ripe honeydew melon or
  1 small ogen melon
1 orange, peeled and divided into
  segments
2·5 cm (1 inch) piece cucumber,
  chopped
1 tbls chopped fresh mint
¼ small lettuce, shredded
15 g (½ oz) toasted almonds or
  hazelnuts
2 mint sprigs, to garnish (optional)

Cut the melon into quarters and remove the seeds. Using a melon baller,
scoop out the flesh, or cut into small
cubes with a knife. Place in a bowl.

Cut the orange segments in half
crossways. Add to the bowl with the
cucumber and mint and toss lightly.
Cover and chill in the refrigerator until
ready to serve.

Divide the lettuce between 2 individual serving dishes or glasses. Spoon
in the melon mixture, pouring over the
juice. Sprinkle with almonds and garnish with mint sprigs if liked

Serving idea: If using an ogen melon,
cut in half and scoop out the seeds.
Scoop out the flesh and mix with the
other ingredients, then serve the melon
cocktail in the melon case.
Variations: Use a few grapes, halved
and seeded, instead of the cucumber.
Add a few drops of kirsch to the cocktail
before chilling.

Deep-fried camembert

4 individual portions ripe camembert
1 egg, beaten
about 100 g (4 oz) dry white
  breadcrumbs
vegetable oil, for deep-frying
a few lettuce leaves, to garnish
cranberry or redcurrant jelly to serve

Dip the camembert portions first in the beaten egg, then in the breadcrumbs, making sure that the cheese is thoroughly coated. Apply a second coating of egg and breadcrumbs. Chill in the refrigerator for 30 minutes.

Heat the oil in a deep-fat fryer to 190°C/375°F, or until a stale bread cube browns in 30 seconds. Deep-fry the camembert portions for about 3 minutes until golden brown on all sides.

Remove with a slotted spoon and drain on absorbent kitchen paper. Place the camembert on a serving platter and garnish with the lettuce leaves. Serve immediately, accompanied by cranberry or redcurrant jelly.

Serving idea: The deep-fried camembert makes a substantial starter, so serve before a light main course.
Variations: Mango chutney makes a tasty accompaniment instead of cranberry jelly. Or serve the deep-fried camembert with a fresh gooseberry sauce. Watercress sprigs make an attractive garnish. You can also use other soft cheeses such as brie.

● Deep-fried camembert; Mushrooms à la grecque

Mushrooms à la grecque

1 tbls olive oil
½ small onion, finely chopped
1 garlic clove, crushed
2 tomatoes, skinned, seeded and
  finely chopped
225 g (8 oz) button mushrooms,
  roughly chopped
2 tsp tomato purée
65 ml (2½ fl oz) dry white wine
2 tbls chopped fresh parsley
salt and pepper

Heat the oil in a frying pan. Add the onion and garlic and fry gently for 5 minutes until softened. Add the tomatoes and mushrooms and cook for a further 5 minutes, stirring occasionally.

Mix the tomato purée with the wine and add to the pan. Bring just to boiling point then remove immediately from the heat and add half the parsley, salt and plenty of pepper. Stir well, transfer to a serving dish and set aside to cool.

Chill in the refrigerator for at least 2 hours before serving. Adjust the seasoning to taste and sprinkle the remaining parsley over the top.

Serving ideas: Serve as part of an hors d'oeuvres with stuffed eggs, tomato salad and sliced salami or on its own with hot French bread for the juices.
Variations: For courgettes à la grecque, use 225 g (8 oz) sliced courgettes instead of mushrooms. For onions à la grecque, use peeled button onions and serve as a vegetable accompaniment or part of a selection of salads, rather than as a starter.

Tomato and mozzarella salad

3 large ripe tomatoes, thinly sliced
100 g (4 oz) mozzarella cheese, thinly
   sliced
3 tbls olive oil
1 tbls lemon juice
1 tbls chopped fresh basil
salt and pepper
8 black olives, stoned, to garnish

Arrange the tomato and mozzarella cheese slices overlapping on 2 individual serving plates.

In a bowl, blend together the olive oil, lemon juice and basil and season to taste. Pour the dressing over the tomatoes and cheese and garnish with the olives.

Serving ideas: Serve this quick-to-prepare starter with Italian breadsticks or hot buttered toast. For a light lunch serve with sliced salami.
Variations: If you have difficulty obtaining fresh basil, use 1 tbls snipped chives instead. Try to buy real Italian mozzarella cheese for this recipe, as it has the best flavour. Or substitute Cheshire cheese.

• Far left: Tomato and mozzarella salad
Left: Prawn and cream cheese pâté

In a bowl, beat the cheese with a wooden spoon until it is smooth. Add the remaining ingredients and beat well. Divide the mixture between individual ramekins. Smooth the tops and garnish with the olives and fennel tops.

Serving idea: Serve with crisp melba toast.
Variation: If you have difficulty obtaining fennel or dill, use snipped chives instead.

Bean salad

198g (7oz) can flageolet beans
198g (7oz) can kidney beans
198g (7oz) can sweetcorn
1/2 red pepper, chopped
3 spring onions, chopped
1 tbls chopped fresh parsley, to
  garnish
For the dressing
1 tbls olive oil
2 tsp lemon juice
1 garlic clove, crushed
1/2 tsp French mustard
1/2 tsp caster sugar
salt and pepper
a few mint leaves, chopped

Drain the beans and sweetcorn. Mix together with the red pepper and spring onions. Combine the ingredients for the dressing in a jug or separate bowl and pour over the salad. Mix well and sprinkle with the chopped parsley. Cover and chill in the refrigerator for 30 minutes before serving.

Variations: Use canned chick peas instead of kidney beans. Any chopped fresh herbs such as tarragon or chives may be included in the dressing.

Prawn and cream cheese pâté

50g (2oz) full fat soft cheese
1 spring onion, very finely chopped
75g (3oz) peeled prawns, chopped
1 tbls lemon juice
salt and pepper
1 tbls finely chopped fresh fennel tops
  or dill
pinch of paprika
pinch of cayenne
To garnish
2 black olives, stoned
fennel tops or dill

● Eggs mimosa

Eggs mimosa

2 hard-boiled eggs, shelled and
· halved lengthways
50 g (2 oz) peeled prawns, chopped
120 ml (4 fl oz) thick mayonnaise
2 tsp hot water
watercress sprigs and whole prawns,
  to garnish

Using a teaspoon, scoop out the egg
yolks. Rub 1 yolk through a fine sieve
into a bowl. Mix in the prawns and stir
in 2 tsp mayonnaise.

Arrange the egg whites cut side up on
a serving dish and fill each half with the
prawn mixture.

Stir the hot water into the remaining
mayonnaise and spoon evenly over the
eggs. Sieve the remaining yolk over the
top and garnish with watercress sprigs
prawn mixture.

Serving idea: Serve with thin slices of
brown bread and butter.
Variation: Replace the prawns with 6
anchovy fillets, soaked in milk then
drained and finely chopped.

Risotto medley

50g (2oz) margarine or butter
½ small onion, chopped
100g (4oz) Italian spiced sausages,
  sliced
50g (2oz) shelled peas
1 artichoke heart, chopped
25g (1oz) mushrooms, chopped
200ml (7fl oz) beef stock
salt and pepper
175g (6oz) rice
500ml (18fl oz) water
3 tbls grated Parmesan cheese
1 tbls chopped fresh parsley

Heat the oven to 160°C. 325°F. Gas Mark 3.

Melt half the margarine in a large flameproof casserole, add the onion and fry gently for 7 minutes until golden. Add the sausages and fry, stirring, for 3 minutes. Add the peas, artichoke, mushrooms, stock and seasoning. Cover and simmer for 20 minutes.

Meanwhile, put the rice and water in a large saucepan, add salt to taste, bring to the boil and boil for 5 minutes. Drain, then add to the vegetable and sausage mixture with the Parmesan and remaining margarine. Mix well.

Put the risotto in the oven for 15 minutes or until heated through. Garnish with the chopped parsley and serve immediately.

Serving idea: Serve with a crisp green salad and red wine for an informal quick supper dish. Or serve as an accompaniment to chicken or pork.

• Risotto medley

Fish kebabs

½ small green pepper, cored and
 seeded
½ small red pepper, cored and seeded
225g (8 oz) cod fillet, skinned and cut
 into 2·5 cm (1 inch) cubes
50g (2 oz) peeled prawns
vegetable oil, for brushing
75g (3 oz) mushrooms, trimmed
1 garlic clove, halved
4 bay leaves
4 small tomatoes
lemon wedges, to garnish (optional)
For the marinade
2 tbls vegetable oil
1 tbls lemon juice
salt and pepper
½ tsp dried oregano

Place the peppers in boiling water and
simmer for 5 minutes. Drain, refresh
under cold running water and drain
again, then cut into 2·5 cm (1 inch)
squares.

Combine all the marinade ingredients in a large bowl. Add the cod,
prawns, peppers and mushrooms and
stir well to mix. Cover and chill in the
refrigerator for 2 hours, stirring the
marinade occasionally.

Heat the grill to moderate. Brush 2
kebab skewers with oil, and rub each
skewer with the cut sides of the garlic
clove. Using a slotted spoon, remove the
kebab ingredients from the marinade,
reserving the marinade.

Thread the pieces of fish, prawns,
peppers, mushrooms, bay leaves and
tomatoes alternately on to the skewers.

Lay the kebabs on the grill rack and
grill for 12 minutes, turning and basting with the reserved marinade several
times during cooking. Serve immediately, garnished with lemon
wedges, if liked.

Serving idea: Serve on a bed of savory
rice with a cucumber or fennel salad.
Variations: For a more pronounced
spicy flavour, add ½ tsp ground coriander to the marinade instead of the dried
oregano. Haddock fillet or any other
firm white fish may replace the cod.

Cod cutlets with savoury stuffing

2 cod cutlets, trimmed and central
 bones removed
2 tbls milk
For the stuffing
15g (½ oz) margarine or butter
½ small onion, finely chopped
2 rashers streaky bacon, rinded and
 chopped
1 tomato, skinned and finely chopped
15g (½ oz) fresh white breadcrumbs
salt and pepper
To garnish
grilled tomatoes
dill sprigs

Heat the oven to 160°C, 325°F, Gas Mark 3. Place the cod cutlets in a greased ovenproof dish.

To make the stuffing, melt the margarine in a small frying pan, add the onion and bacon and fry gently for 5 minutes until the onion is softened. Add the tomato and breadcrumbs, season with salt and pepper and stir to mix thoroughly.

Using a teaspoon, spoon the stuffing into the centre of each cutlet. Pour the milk around the fish, cover tightly and cook in the oven for about 20 minutes, until the cod is tender. Transfer the cutlets to a heated serving dish, garnish with grilled tomatoes and dill sprigs and serve immediately.

Serving ideas: Serve with sauté potatoes and peas, or creamed potatoes and runner beans.

Variations: Omit the tomato and add the grated rind and juice of 1 lemon or small orange to the stuffing mixture. A small dessert apple or a large celery stalk, finely chopped, may also replace the tomato. Wholemeal breadcrumbs may be used instead of white.

● Fish kebabs
Cod cutlets with savoury stuffing

Stir-fried chicken with peppers

1 egg white
2 tsp cornflour
½ tsp salt
225 g (8 oz) chicken breast, skinned,
  boned and cut into 1 cm (½ inch)
  cubes
3 tbls vegetable oil
2 spring onions, cut into 2·5 cm (1
  inch) lengths
3 dried red chillis, soaked in water,
  drained and chopped
50 g (2 oz) roasted peanuts, finely
  chopped
chopped spring onion tops, to garnish
For the sauce
1 tbls sugar
1 tbls white wine vinegar
1½ tsp cornflour
1 tbls water

Lightly whisk the egg white with the cornflour and salt in a bowl. Add the chicken and stir to coat thoroughly. Combine the sauce ingredients in a separate small bowl.

Heat the oil in a frying pan, add the coated chicken and stir-fry for 2-3 minutes until lightly coloured, then remove with a slotted spoon and set aside on a plate.

Add the spring onions and chillis to the pan, stir-fry for 1-2 minutes, then add the peanuts and return the chicken to the pan with the sauce mixture. Stir-fry for 1-2 minutes, then pile on to a heated serving dish, sprinkle with the chopped spring onion tops and serve immediately.

Serving ideas: Serve with fried rice and a beansprout salad or lightly cooked French beans.
Variation: Use 225 g (8 oz) pork fillet or frying steak instead of the chicken breast.

Nutty lamb cutlets

4 lamb best end of neck cutlets
25 g (1 oz) plain flour
1 egg, beaten
25 g (1 oz) walnuts or hazelnuts,
   finely chopped
15 g (½ oz) cornflakes, crushed
2 tbls vegetable oil
To garnish
watercress sprigs
tomato wedges

Coat the cutlets in the flour, then dip in
the beaten egg. Mix the walnuts with
the cornflakes and press the cutlets
into the mixture, to coat thoroughly
and evenly on both sides.

Heat the oil in a frying pan, add the
cutlets and fry over a moderately high
heat for 8-10 minutes, turning once,
until golden brown and tender. Transfer the cutlets to a heated serving dish,
garnish with watercress sprigs and
tomato wedges and serve immediately.

Serving ideas: Serve with new potatoes and creamed spinach, and hand
mint sauce or redcurrant jelly
separately.
Variation: Use salted peanuts instead
of the walnuts or hazelnuts.

• Stir-fried chicken with peppers
Nutty lamb cutlets

Curried aubergines

2 small aubergines
2 tbls vegetable oil
salt and pepper
1 small onion, chopped
50 g (2 oz) mushrooms, chopped
1 garlic clove, crushed
75 g (3 oz) cooked ham, finely
    chopped
½ tsp curry powder
1 tbls tomato purée
1 tsp Worcestershire sauce

Heat the oven to 190°C, 375°F, Gas Mark 5. Cut the aubergines in half lengthways. Score the cut surfaces with a sharp knife, taking care not to break the skin. Rub the scored surfaces with ½ tbls oil and salt, then place the aubergine halves, cut side uppermost, on a greased baking sheet. Bake in the oven for 15 minutes or until tender.

Using a teaspoon, scoop the aubergine flesh into a bowl, reserving the 'shells'. Heat all but 1 tsp of the remaining oil in a frying pan, add the onion and mushrooms and fry gently for 3 minutes.

Add the garlic and aubergine flesh and fry together, stirring, for a further 2 minutes, until the vegetables are soft. Add the ham, curry powder, tomato purée and Worcestershire sauce and season to taste. Stir well to mix.

Pile the mixture into the aubergine shells and replace on the baking sheet. Sprinkle with the remaining oil and bake in the oven for 25-30 minutes until golden brown.

Spicy rice salad

2 tsp vegetable oil
1 small onion, chopped
75 g (3 oz) long-grain rice
salt and pepper
75 g (3 oz) cabanos sausage, chopped
½ small red pepper, cored, seeded
   and chopped
50 g (2 oz) button mushrooms, sliced
1 tsp lemon juice
2 tbls thick mayonnaise
pinch of paprika
2 tsp snipped chives, to garnish

Heat the oil in a small pan, add the onion, and fry gently for 7 minutes until golden. Remove with a slotted spoon and drain on absorbent kitchen paper.

Meanwhile, cook the rice in boiling salted water for about 20 minutes or until tender. Drain and rinse under cold running water then drain again. Place in a salad bowl and mix in the onion, sausage, pepper, mushrooms and lemon juice.

Add the mayonnaise with the paprika and toss until all the ingredients are thoroughly coated. Season to taste. Sprinkle with the chives before serving.

Variation: Use diced cooked leftover chicken instead of sausage.

• Curried aubergines; Spicy rice salad

• Salad niçoise; Spaghetti with tuna sauce

Salad niçoise

½ crisp Cos lettuce, divided into
  leaves
2 celery stalks, chopped
2 tomatoes, skinned, seeded and
  chopped
½ green pepper, cored, seeded and
  chopped
99 g (3½ oz) can tuna fish, drained
  and flaked
56 g (2 oz) can anchovies, drained
  and soaked in milk for 30 minutes,
  then drained again
1 hard-boiled egg, shelled and
  quartered
25 g (1 oz) black olives, stoned
5 tbls French dressing

Line a salad bowl with the lettuce
leaves. Place the celery, tomatoes and
pepper in the bowl, then add the tuna.
Stir lightly to mix.

Arrange the anchovies in a lattice
pattern over the top of the salad. Garnish with the egg quarters and olives.
Sprinkle French dressing over the
salad just before serving.

Serving idea: Serve the salad as a delicious summer meal in itself with warm
herb bread and chilled white or rosé
wine.

Variations: Add 50 g (2 oz) cooked cold
French beans to the salad instead of the
celery. For an even more substantial
salad, add some sliced cooked potatoes.

24

Spaghetti with tuna sauce

salt and pepper
1 tsp vegetable oil
175 g (6 oz) spaghetti
25 g (1 oz) butter
1 tbls olive oil
1 garlic clove, finely chopped
100 ml (3½ fl oz) chicken stock
2 tbls dry sherry
99 g (3½ oz) can tuna fish, drained
*   and flaked*
1½ tbls chopped fresh parsley
1 tbls single cream

Bring a large saucepan of salted water to the boil and add the vegetable oil. Add the spaghetti and cook for about 12 minutes or until just tender. Drain,

return to the pan and stir in half the butter, then cover and keep warm.

Meanwhile, heat the olive oil and remaining butter in a saucepan. Add the garlic and fry over moderate heat for 2 minutes. Pour on the stock and sherry and boil rapidly for 5 minutes to reduce.

Add the tuna fish and 1 tbls parsley. Stir to mix, season, and stir in the cream. Turn the spaghetti into a heated serving dish, pour on the sauce and toss lightly. Sprinkle with the remaining parsley.

Serving idea: Serve with a refreshing tomato salad sprinkled with chopped fresh basil.
Variation: Add 1 tbls stoned, chopped black olives to the spaghetti with the tuna sauce.

Eggs Greek style

1 small aubergine, thinly sliced
salt and pepper
3 tbls vegetable oil
1 small onion, chopped
½ green pepper, cored, seeded and
  diced
2 tomatoes, skinned, seeded and
  chopped
1 back bacon rasher, rinded and
  chopped
2 eggs

Place the aubergine slices in a colander and sprinkle with salt. Leave to stand for 30 minutes. Rinse under cold running water, drain again and pat dry with absorbent kitchen paper.

Heat ½ tbls oil in a frying pan. Add the onion and pepper and fry gently for 5 minutes until softened. Remove with a slotted spoon and set aside on a plate.

Heat a further 2 tbls oil in the pan, add the aubergine slices and fry over a moderate heat, turning once, for 5-10 minutes until browned on both sides. Remove with a slotted spoon and drain on absorbent kitchen paper.

Return the drained aubergines to the pan with the onion and pepper and stir in the tomatoes. Season and cook gently for a further 5 minutes. Spoon the vegetable mixture into a heated serving dish and keep warm.

Meanwhile, fry the bacon in the pan until well browned, then remove from the pan with a slotted spoon. Fry the eggs and arrange over the vegetable mixture. Sprinkle with the bacon pieces and serve immediately.

Serving idea: Serve for lunch or supper with crusty wholemeal bread.
Variation: Use 225 g (8 oz) courgettes instead of the aubergine.

● Eggs Greek style
Liver with sage

Liver with sage

15 g (½ oz) butter
1 tsp vegetable oil
225 g (8 oz) lamb's liver, thinly sliced
1 small onion, chopped
25 g (1 oz) button mushrooms, sliced
1 tsp plain flour
100 ml (3½ fl oz) beef stock
50 ml (2 fl oz) red wine
2 tsp chopped fresh sage or 1 tsp dried
  sage
salt and pepper
fresh sage leaves, to garnish

Heat the butter and oil in a frying pan, add the liver and fry quickly over a high heat for 2-3 minutes, turning once, until light golden brown. Remove from the pan and keep warm.

Reduce the heat, add the onion to the pan and fry gently for 3 minutes. Add the mushrooms and cook for a further 3 minutes until the onion is softened.

Remove the pan from the heat and sprinkle in the flour. Stir well to mix. Return to the heat and gradually stir in the stock and wine. Add the sage and season to taste.

Return the liver to the pan and simmer gently for 8-10 minutes until tender. Transfer the liver to a heated serving dish, pour over the sauce and garnish with the sage leaves.

Serving ideas: Serve with sauté or boiled new potatoes and French beans or broccoli spears. Or instead of potatoes, try small haricot beans boiled, buttered and garnished with parsley.

Variation: For a special occasion, use calf's liver, which is more expensive but has a particularly delicious flavour.

Curried prawns with spinach

1 tbls vegetable oil
1 onion, thinly sliced
1 garlic clove, cut into slivers
2 tsp tomato purée
¼ tsp garam masala
1 tsp ground coriander
½ tsp ground cumin
¼ tsp ground turmeric
¼ tsp chilli powder
¼ tsp ground ginger
½ tsp salt
225 g (8 oz) frozen chopped spinach
225 g (8 oz) peeled prawns
fresh coriander leaves, to garnish

Heat the oil in a heavy-based saucepan, add the onion and garlic and fry gently for 5 minutes until softened. Stir in the tomato purée and fry, stirring, for 1 minute. Add the spices and salt and fry for a further 5 minutes, stirring constantly.

Add the spinach and break up with a wooden spoon. Cook until the spinach has thawed completely, stirring frequently, then add the prawns. Cook for a further 5 minutes, turning the prawns gently to coat with the spinach mixture.

Pile into a heated serving dish, garnish with coriander leaves and serve immediately.

Serving idea: Serve with boiled rice, banana slices dipped in lemon juice, cucumber pickle and poppadoms.

Sole with whisky sauce

40g (1½oz) butter
1 large Dover or lemon sole, divided
   into 4 fillets and skinned
½ small fennel bulb, thinly sliced
1 garlic clove, crushed
2 tbls whisky
50g (2oz) peeled prawns
1 large, firm tomato, skinned, seeded
   and chopped
85 ml (3 fl oz) double cream
salt and pepper
4 whole unpeeled prawns, to garnish

Melt 25 g (1 oz) of the butter in a large frying pan. Add the sole fillets in a single layer and fry very gently for 2-3 minutes on each side until cooked through but not browned. Using a fish slice, transfer to a heated serving dish and keep warm while making the sauce.

Melt the remaining butter in the pan, add the fennel and garlic and fry gently for 5-10 minutes, stirring occasionally, until softened.

Raise the heat, add the whisky and stir until reduced slightly, then lower the heat and stir in the prawns and tomato. Simmer gently for 5 minutes, then stir in the cream. Heat through, then add seasoning to taste.

Remove the prawn and tomato mixture from the pan with a slotted spoon and spoon over the sole fillets. Pour over the remaining sauce, garnish with the whole prawns and serve immediately.

Serving idea: Serve with sauté potatoes and courgettes.
Variation: Use 4 small or 2 large plaice fillets instead of the sole.

• Curried prawns with spinach; Sole with whisky sauce

Mackerel with lemon and orange stuffing

• Mackerel with lemon and orange stuffing; Smoked haddock soufflé

2 medium mackerel, cleaned and
*   gutted*
lemon and orange slices, to garnish
For the stuffing
1 orange, peeled and roughly
*   chopped*
½ small onion, finely chopped
25 g (1 oz) fresh white breadcrumbs
2 tsp chopped fresh parsley
finely grated rind of ½ lemon
1 tbls lemon juice
salt and pepper
parsley sprigs

Heat the oven to 160°C, 325°F, Gas Mark 3. Line an ovenproof dish with buttered foil.

Place all the stuffing ingredients in a bowl and stir well to mix. Spoon the stuffing into the mackerel and place in the dish.

Cover loosely with foil and cook in the oven for 30-35 minutes or until the mackerel is cooked through and flakes easily when pierced with a sharp knife.

Transfer the mackerel to a heated serving dish. Pour the cooking juices over the fish, garnish with lemon and orange slices and parsley sprigs and serve immediately.

Serving idea: Serve with buttered new potatoes or brown bread and butter and a green salad or sliced tomato salad.

Variation: Rainbow trout may be used instead of mackerel.

Smoked haddock soufflé

225 g (8 oz) smoked haddock fillet
150 ml (¼ pint) milk
15 g (½ oz) margarine or butter
15 g (½ oz) plain flour
2 eggs, separated
salt and pepper

Heat the oven to 200°C, 400°F, Gas Mark 6. Place the smoked haddock in a large frying pan with a lid. Pour over the milk and bring gently to the boil. Cover and simmer for 10 minutes until the haddock is cooked through. Remove from the heat and set aside for 5-10 minutes, then drain, reserving the milk. Flake the haddock, discarding any skin and bones, and mash the flesh with a fork.

Place margarine, flour and reserved milk in a saucepan. Bring to the boil over a high heat, whisking continuously until thickened. Simmer for 2 minutes. Remove from the heat. Add the mashed haddock, egg yolks, salt if necessary and plenty of freshly ground black pepper.

Whisk the egg whites stiffly and fold into the mixture, using a large metal spoon.

Turn the mixture into a lightly greased 900 ml (1½ pint) soufflé dish and bake in the oven for about 20 minutes, until well risen and golden brown. Serve the smoked haddock soufflé immediately.

Serving idea: Serve with crusty bread and a green salad for a tasty supper dish.
Variations: For a kipper soufflé use 225 g (8 oz) kipper fillets instead of the haddock. Or make a smoked trout soufflé.

31

Beef stifado

25 g (1 oz) plain flour
salt and pepper
350 g (12 oz) lean chuck steak,
 trimmed and cut into 2·5 cm (1 inch)
 cubes
2 tbls vegetable oil
¼ tsp cumin seeds
2·5 cm (1 inch) piece cinnamon stick
1 tbls tomato purée
1 tbls herb vinegar
300 ml (½ pint) beef stock
2 sprigs fresh thyme
100 g (4 oz) button onions, peeled but
 left whole
50 g (2 oz) feta cheese, crumbled
2 tsp chopped fresh parsley, to garnish

Heat the oven to 160°C, 325°F, Gas
Mark 3. Season the flour and use to
dust the beef cubes.

Heat the oil in a large frying pan, add
the beef and fry over a moderately high
heat, turning, for 3-4 minutes, until
the meat is browned on all sides. Transfer to a casserole with a slotted spoon.

Add the cumin, cinnamon stick and
tomato purée to the pan. Stir in the
vinegar, stock and thyme, and adjust
the seasoning to taste. Bring to the boil.

Pour the sauce over the meat, cover
and cook in the oven for 2 hours.

Plunge the onions into boiling water
for 3 minutes, drain and add to the
casserole. Cook for a further 30 minutes or until the meat is tender. Add
the cheese to the casserole and return
uncovered to the oven for a few minutes, until the cheese begins to melt.
Sprinkle with the parsley and serve immediately.

Serving idea: Serve with baked potatoes and a mixed salad.
Variation: Rabbit may be used instead
of beef in this traditional Greek recipe.

Minute steak with mushrooms

2 thin-cut sirloin steaks, each
 weighing 100-175 g (4-6 oz)
1 garlic clove, halved (optional)
pepper
2 tsp vegetable oil
40 g (1½ oz) butter
salt
175 g (6 oz) button mushrooms, thinly
 sliced
2 tbls soured cream
1 tbls lemon juice
2 tsp snipped chives
2 tsp chopped fresh parsley
watercress sprigs, to garnish

● Beef stifado
Minute steak with mushrooms

Pat the steaks dry with absorbent kitchen paper. Rub each side of the steaks with the cut side of the garlic, if using, and season with freshly ground black pepper.

Heat the oil and half the butter in a large frying pan. When the foam subsides, add the steaks and cook over a moderately high heat for 2 minutes on each side for medium steak, or a little longer for well done steak. Season with salt. Transfer the steaks to a heated serving dish and keep hot while preparing the sauce.

Heat the remaining butter in the pan and add the mushrooms. Reduce the heat and cook, stirring, for a few minutes until the mushrooms begin to soften. Stir in the soured cream and lemon juice and a little salt, then spoon the mushrooms and their juices over the steaks. Sprinkle with the herbs, garnish with watercress sprigs and serve immediately.

Serving idea: Serve with French fries and a green salad or sauté potatoes and ratatouille. Also good with this dish are glazed carrots and tiny onions.

Variations: Omit the soured cream for a less rich dish. Veal escalopes or slices of pork tenderloin beaten out finely may be cooked in the same way. For a more economical dish use frying steak or hamburgers instead of the sirloin steak.

Honeyed shoulder of pork with red cabbage

1 tbls vegetable oil
750 g (1 ½ lb) shoulder of pork
15 g (½ oz) margarine or butter
1 small onion, sliced
½ small red cabbage, shredded
5 tbls red wine
5 tbls chicken stock
salt and pepper
1 tbls clear honey
1 tbls chopped fresh parsley, to garnish

Heat the oven to 180°C, 350°F, Gas Mark 4. Heat the oil in a large frying pan, add the pork and fry over a high heat, turning, for 3-4 minutes until browned on all sides. Remove from the pan and set aside on a plate.

Melt the margarine in the pan, add the onion and fry gently for 5 minutes until softened, then transfer to a casserole.

Blanch the cabbage by placing it in boiling water for 3 minutes. Drain well and place in the casserole with the onion. Pour over the red wine and stock and season well.

Spread the honey over the pork rind and place pork on the vegetable mixture. Cover and cook in the oven for 1-1¼ hours until cooked through. Adjust the seasoning to taste and serve straight from the casserole, with the pork carved into thick slices, garnished with chopped parsley.

Serving idea: Serve with baked potatoes with soured cream and chives.
Variation: Fry 1 small apple, peeled and sliced, with the onion and add to the casserole.

● Honeyed shoulder of pork with red cabbage; Apple and Stilton pork

Apple and Stilton pork

15 g (½ oz) butter
2 boneless pork steaks, about 175 g
(6 oz) each
50 g (2 oz) Stilton cheese, grated
1 red dessert apple
5 tbls dry white wine
5 tbls double cream
salt and pepper
2 tsp chopped fresh parsley, to garnish

Melt the butter in a frying pan, add the pork steaks and fry over a moderate heat for 15-20 minutes, turning once, until cooked through. Transfer to an ovenproof serving dish and keep warm.

Place the grated cheese in a small mixing bowl. Core and finely chop half the apple, leaving the skin on, and add to the cheese with 2 tbls of the wine and 1 tbls of the cream. Spoon the mixture over the pork steaks and place under a hot grill until the topping is bubbling and golden brown.

Meanwhile, slice the remaining apple thinly and add to the frying pan with the remaining wine. Season and simmer gently for 2-3 minutes until the apple slices are tender. Stir in the remaining cream and bring to the boil.

Pour the sauce over the pork steaks, sprinkle with the parsley and serve immediately.

Variation: Use 50 g (2 oz) grated Parmesan or mature Cheddar cheese instead of the Stilton.

French roast leg of lamb

This recipe will serve four or serve two and provide leftovers which can be used in the Lamb fricassee (page 37). To serve two without leftovers, buy 750 g (1½ lb) fillet end leg of lamb and reduce the cooking time to 45-60 minutes.

1·5 kg (3-3½ lb) leg of lamb
1 garlic clove, cut into slivers
20 g (¾ oz) dripping or lard, melted
salt and pepper
1 small carrot, sliced
1 small onion, quartered
300 ml (½ pint) beef stock
mint sprigs, to garnish

Heat the oven to 230°C, 450°F, Gas Mark 8. Using a small sharp knife, make incisions over the fat surface of the lamb and insert a garlic sliver into each one. Brush the joint with the fat and season.

Place the lamb on a rack in a roasting tin and roast on the top shelf of the oven for 15 minutes, basting occasionally, until the lamb is browned.

Add the carrot and the onion to the tin, under the rack, and transfer to the centre of the oven. Reduce the heat to 180°C, 350°F, Gas Mark 4 and roast for 1-1¼ hours, or until the juices run pink when the lamb is pierced with a fine skewer.

Remove the lamb from the tin and transfer to a heated serving platter. Set aside for 15 minutes in a warm place.

Drain the excess fat from the tin and mash the vegetables with a fork. Pour in the stock and bring to the boil over high heat, stirring constantly to mix all the meat juices into the gravy. Season to taste with salt and pepper.

To serve, carve the lamb into slices, garnish the platter with mint sprigs and hand the gravy separately in a heated gravy boat.

Serving idea: Serve the lamb with new or roast potatoes and minted garden peas and glazed carrots. Hand redcurrant jelly or mint sauce separately if liked.

Variation: Use 5 tbls beef stock mixed with 5 tbls red wine for an especially tasty gravy.

● French roast leg of lamb
Lamb fricassee

Lamb fricassee

This recipe suggests using cooked lamb which could be left over from the French roast leg of lamb on page 36. Alternatively, use the same quantity of uncooked lamb leg steak, trimmed, cubed and tossed in seasoned flour; brown it for 2-3 minutes with the sautéed onion and carrot and cook in the oven for 1¼ hours before adding the mushrooms.

25 g (1 oz) margarine or butter
1 onion, sliced
1 large carrot, sliced
25 g (1 oz) plain flour
300 ml (½ pint) hot chicken stock
350 g (12 oz) cooked lamb, sliced or
*   trimmed and cut into 2·5 cm (1 inch)*
*   cubes*
1 bay leaf
½ tsp chopped fresh thyme or a pinch
*   of dried thyme*
salt and pepper
50 g (2 oz) mushrooms, sliced
1 tbls single cream
thyme sprigs, to garnish

Heat the oven to 180°C, 350°F. Gas Mark 4. Melt the margarine in a flameproof casserole, add the onion and carrot and fry gently for 5 minutes until softened but not coloured.

Sprinkle in the flour and cook for 1 minute, stirring continuously. Gradually stir in the stock and bring to the boil. Add the lamb, bay leaf and thyme, season to taste with salt and pepper, cover and cook in the oven for 25-30 minutes, or until heated through.

Stir in the mushrooms and cook for a further 15 minutes. Remove the bay leaf, stir in the cream and garnish with sprigs of thyme. Serve straight from the casserole.

Serving ideas: Serve with creamed potatoes and buttered leeks, or a rice pilau and a green salad.
Variation: For veal fricassee use 350 g (12 oz) uncooked pie veal and follow the instruction on using uncooked meat at the head of this recipe.

Chicken in egg and lemon sauce

2 chicken pieces, skinned
grated rind of ½ lemon
1 small onion, thinly sliced
1 bay leaf
300 ml (½ pint) chicken stock
a few parsley stalks
salt and white pepper
1 tbls thin strips lemon rind and
    chopped fresh parsley, to garnish
For the sauce
15 g (½ oz) margarine or butter
15 g (½ oz) plain flour
150 ml (¼ pint) milk
1 egg yolk, lightly beaten
1 tbls chopped fresh parsley
1 tbls lemon juice

Put the chicken pieces in a large shallow saucepan with the lemon rind, onion, bay leaf, stock and parsley stalks. Season to taste. Bring to the boil, cover and simmer for 45 minutes or until the chicken is tender. Transfer the chicken to a heated serving dish and keep warm while making the sauce.

To make the sauce, strain the chicken cooking liquid. Place the margarine, flour, milk and 150 ml (¼ pint) of the cooking liquid in a saucepan. Bring to the boil, whisking until thickened.

Season to taste, then stir in the egg yolk, parsley and lemon juice. Heat through gently without allowing the sauce to boil. Pour the sauce over the chicken and garnish with the lemon rind and chopped parsley. Serve immediately.

Serving idea: Serve with buttered noodles and a green salad.
Variation: For a special occasion, omit the milk and combine 5 tbls double cream with the egg yolk before stirring into the sauce.

Greek grilled chicken

2 chicken pieces
for the marinade
3 tbls olive oil
3 tbls lemon juice
strip of thinly pared lemon rind
4 black peppercorns, lightly crushed
1 garlic clove, crushed
1 tsp salt
To garnish
lettuce leaves
lemon wedges

Wipe the chicken pieces with absorbent kitchen paper. Combine all the marinade ingredients in a deep dish. Add the chicken pieces, turn to coat in the marinade, then cover and refrigerate for at least 4 hours, turning the chicken once or twice.

Heat the grill to moderate. Drain the chicken pieces, reserving the marinade. Place the chicken, cut side uppermost, in the grill pan. Grill for 12-15 minutes, basting frequently with the marinade.

Turn, brush with the marinade, and grill for another 12-15 minutes, until the chicken is golden and cooked through and the juices run clear when the thickest part of the thigh is pierced with a skewer.

Place the chicken on a heated serving dish and garnish with lettuce leaves and lemon wedges. Serve immediately.

Serving idea: Serve with a cucumber and yoghurt salad or a Greek salad of lettuce, chopped cucumber, tomato, spring onions, olives and feta cheese, and warm pitta bread.

Variation: Instead of chicken use 2 lamb leg steaks, each weighing about 175 g (6 oz). Grill for a total time of 15 minutes, turning once. Both the lamb and the chicken are delicious grilled on a barbecue.

• Top right: Greek grilled chicken; Bottom right: Chicken in egg and lemon sauce

Normandy chicken

25 g (1 oz) margarine or butter
2 chicken pieces
salt and pepper
350 g (12 oz) dessert apples, peeled,
  cored and sliced
1 tbls lemon juice
1 tbls cider
½ tsp ground cinnamon
15 g (½ oz) seedless raisins, soaked in
  warm water for 1 hour, then
  drained
5 tbls double cream
To garnish
½ red dessert apple, sliced
2 tsp chopped fresh parsley

Heat the oven to 160°C, 325°F, Gas Mark 3.

Melt half the margarine in a frying pan, add the chicken pieces and fry over a moderate heat, turning, for 3-4 minutes, until browned on all sides. Remove the chicken to a plate and season well.

Melt the remaining margarine in the pan, add the apple slices and toss gently for 2-3 minutes until they are lightly coloured.

Place half the apple slices in a casserole and place the chicken on top. Mix together the lemon juice, cider, cinnamon and raisins, and season. Place the remaining apple slices round the chicken, season and pour over the raisin mixture.

Cover with a piece of greaseproof paper or foil and a tight-fitting lid, and cook in the oven for about 1 hour, until the chicken is cooked through. Stir in the cream, add the apple garnish and return to the oven to heat through for 5 minutes. Adjust the seasoning to taste, garnish with chopped parsley and serve immediately, straight from the casserole.

Serving ideas: For a special occasion serve with potato croquettes and French beans. A dry white wine is an ideal accompaniment to this dish.
Variation: For Normandy pork, use 2 pork chops instead of chicken.

Kidneys stroganoff

225 g (8 oz) lambs' kidneys, skinned
  and cored, soaked in cold water for
  30 minutes
½ tbls vegetable oil
25 g (1 oz) butter
1 onion, thinly sliced
75 g (3 oz) button mushrooms, thinly
  sliced
salt and pepper
1 tbls dry white vermouth
65 ml (2½ fl oz) soured cream
2 tsp chopped fresh parsley, to garnish

● Normandy chicken; Kidneys stroganoff

Drain the kidneys and slice as thinly as possible.

Heat the oil with half the butter in a large frying pan, add the onion and fry gently for about 5 minutes until softened. Add the mushrooms and cook gently, stirring, for a further 2-3 minutes.

Increase the heat, add the remaining butter and, when melted, add the sliced kidneys. Cook over moderately high heat for about 5 minutes, turning the kidneys frequently until browned. Pour in the vermouth and boil for 1-2 minutes, then reduce the heat to very low and stir in the soured cream. Season to taste. Simmer gently for 3-5 minutes, stirring from time to time, but do not let it boil.

Transfer to a heated serving dish, sprinkle with chopped parsley and serve immediately.

Neapolitan veal rolls

4 small veal escalopes each 40-45 g
  (1½-2 oz)
40 g (1½ oz) cooked ham, very thinly
  sliced
2 tsp olive oil
15 g (½ oz) butter
5 tbls dry white wine
parsley sprigs and tomato wedges, to
  garnish
For the stuffing
25 g (1 oz) Gruyère cheese, finely
  chopped
25 g (1 oz) sultanas
15 g (½ oz) pine nuts or blanched,
  slivered almonds
25 g (1 oz) chopped fresh parsley
salt and pepper

Lay the veal escalopes between 2 sheets of cling film or damp greaseproof paper and beat them with a rolling pin until very thin. Remove the top layer of cling film or paper and lay a small slice of ham on each piece of veal.

Combine all the stuffing ingredients in a bowl and stir well to mix. Spread the stuffing over the veal escalopes, dividing it equally among them, then roll up and tie in several places with fine string.

Heat the oil with the butter in a frying pan, add the veal rolls and fry over moderately high heat, turning, for 3-4 minutes until lightly browned all over. Pour in the wine, cover tightly and simmer very gently for 20-25 minutes until tender, turning once during cooking.

Transfer the veal rolls to a heated serving dish, remove the string and keep hot. Boil the pan juices rapidly until reduced and slightly syrupy, then pour over the rolls. Garnish with parsley sprigs and tomato wedges and serve immediately.

Serving idea: Serve with creamed potatoes and broccoli spears.

Variations: For a different-flavoured stuffing, use 1 tbls fresh white bread-crumbs and the grated rind of ½ lemon instead of the sultanas and nuts. Turkey escalopes can also be used.

Veal escalopes milanese

2 veal escalopes, each about 100 g
  (4 oz)
1 egg, beaten
about 50 g (2 oz) dried breadcrumbs
40 g (1½ oz) butter
salt and pepper
To garnish
lemon slices
savory sprigs

Lay the veal escalopes between 2 sheets of cling film or damp greaseproof paper and beat them out thinly with a rolling pin. Dip first into the egg then into the breadcrumbs to coat evenly.

Melt the butter in a large frying pan, add the escalopes and fry over a moderate heat for 2-3 minutes on each side until tender and golden brown.

Transfer to a heated serving dish and season to taste. Garnish with lemon slices and savory sprigs and serve immediately.

Serving idea: Serve with spaghetti and a fresh tomato sauce.

Variations: Replace the veal with 8 oz (225 g) pork fillet, cut into two equal pieces and beaten to flatten. Garnish the escalopes with any seasonal herb of your choice.

● Neapolitan veal rolls
Veal escalopes milanese

• Cottage cheese and spinach quiche

Cottage cheese and spinach quiche

For the pastry
100g (4oz) plain flour
pinch of salt
25g (1 oz) margarine or butter, diced
25g (1 oz) lard, diced
cold water, to mix
For the filling
100g (4oz) spinach
113g (4oz) carton cottage cheese
1 egg, beaten
3 tbls single cream or milk
pinch of grated nutmeg
1 tbls grated Parmesan cheese
salt and pepper
1 hard-boiled egg, sliced, to garnish

Heat the oven to 200°C, 400°F, Gas Mark 6.

To make the pastry, sift the flour with the salt into a mixing bowl. Add the fats and rub in with the fingertips until the mixture resembles fine breadcrumbs, then add enough water to ·mix to a pliable dough.

Roll out the dough on a lightly floured surface and use to line a 15 cm (6 inch) flan ring. Chill in the refrigerator while making the filling.

Thoroughly wash the spinach and place in a saucepan. Cook without added water for about 5 minutes, covered, until just tender. Drain thoroughly and chop finely.

In a bowl, combine the spinach, cottage cheese, egg, cream, nutmeg, Parmesan cheese and salt and pepper to taste, then pour into the pastry case.

Bake in the oven for about 30 minutes until the filling is firm to the touch and the pastry is golden. Garnish with egg slices and serve hot or cold.

Serving idea: Serve with a tomato and basil salad.
Variation: Use full fat soft cheese or curd cheese instead of cottage cheese.

Spicy poached peaches

25 g (1 oz) butter
50 g (2 oz) soft light brown sugar
65 ml (2½ fl oz) sweet white wine
piece of cinnamon stick
2 medium or 4 small peaches,
*   skinned, halved and stoned*
1½ tsp cornflour
2 tbls water
2 tsp brandy

Place the butter, sugar, wine and cinnamon in a large saucepan and stir over a low heat until the sugar dissolves. Bring slowly to simmering point and add the peaches. Simmer for 5 minutes until tender. Lift out the peaches and place in a heated serving dish. Discard the cinnamon stick.

Blend the cornflour with the water to make a smooth paste, then stir into the syrup in the pan and bring to the boil, stirring constantly, until the sauce thickens. Cook, stirring, for a further 2 minutes, then remove from the heat and stir in the brandy. Pour over the peaches and serve.

Serving idea: Serve warm with single cream or vanilla ice cream.
Variation: Use other fruit such as nectarines or pears or 225 g (8 oz) stoned apricots or plums, increasing the cooking time as necessary until the fruit is tender.

• Spicy poached peaches

Poor knights

4 thin slices white bread
50 g (2 oz) full fat soft cheese
2 tbls sultanas
2 tbls demerara sugar
1 egg
2 tbls single cream
40 g (1½ oz) butter

Spread each bread slice on one side with the cheese. Sprinkle half the slices with the sultanas and sugar. Cover with the remaining slices, cheese side down. Press firmly together, cut off the crusts and cut each sandwich in half.

Beat the egg with the cream in a shallow bowl. Heat the butter in a large frying pan until sizzling. Dip the sandwiches into the beaten egg and cream mixture, then add to the pan.

Fry over a low heat, turning once, for 6-8 minutes until crisp and golden. Remove from the pan and drain quickly on absorbent kitchen paper. Arrange on a heated serving dish and serve immediately.

Serving idea: Serve with a jam sauce: heat 3 tbls apricot or strawberry jam with 1 tbls water in a small saucepan while frying the sandwiches.

● Poor knights; Apple crisps; Cassata cheese

Cassata cheese

100 g (4 oz) full fat soft cheese
40 g (1½ oz) caster sugar
grated rind of ½ orange
grated rind of ½ lemon
100 ml (3½ fl oz) double cream,
*   whipped*
40 g (1½ oz) almonds, toasted and
*   chopped*
25 g (1 oz) glacé cherries, chopped
1 canned (or fresh) pineapple ring,
*   drained and chopped*
shredded orange zest, to decorate

Beat the cheese in a bowl with the caster sugar and fruit rinds until light and fluffy. Fold in the whipped cream, nuts, cherries and pineapple. Spoon the mixture into 2 ramekin dishes and chill in the refrigerator for 2-3 hours. Decorate with shredded orange zest.

Serving idea: Serve with sponge fingers, macaroons or langue de chat.

Apple crisps

2 cooking apples, peeled, cored and
*   sliced*
2 tbls water
caster sugar, to taste
4 tbls double cream
15 g (½ oz) margarine or butter
1 tbls golden syrup
20 g (¾ oz) cornflakes

Place the apples and water in a saucepan. Cover and simmer gently for about 10 minutes until the apples are soft and pulpy. Add sugar to taste and set aside to cool.

Spoon the stewed apple into 2 glasses. Whip the cream until thick and spoon over the fruit.

Melt the margarine in a saucepan. Stir in the syrup, then add the cornflakes. Stir well to mix, then remove from the heat and set aside to cool. Spoon the cornflake mixture over the cream in the glasses.

Variation: Stew 100 g (4 oz) blackberries or raspberries with the apple.

Ginger soufflé omelette

*1 small piece preserved stem ginger,
  chopped*
2 tbls ginger marmalade
3 eggs, separated
1½ tbls caster sugar
15 g (½ oz) butter
2 tsp icing sugar, sifted

Heat the grill to moderate. Stir the chopped ginger into the marmalade. Beat the egg yolks with the sugar in a bowl until pale and creamy. Whisk the egg whites stiffly, then fold into the egg yolk mixture.

Melt the butter in a large frying pan and when sizzling pour in the egg mixture, spreading it out to cover the base of the pan evenly. Cook over moderate heat for about 3 minutes, or until the underside of the omelette is golden brown.

Place under the grill for 2 minutes or until firm and brown on top. Spread the omelette with the marmalade mixture and grill for 1 further minute, until melted and bubbling.

Sprinkle the top with the icing sugar. Serve the omelette immediately, cut into wedges.

Serving idea: Serve with scoops of vanilla ice cream.
Variation: Use lime marmalade or apricot jam instead of the ginger marmalade and omit the stem ginger.

● Ginger soufflé omelette; Hot fruit salad

Hot fruit salad

15 g (½ oz) soft light brown sugar
300 ml (½ pint) water
2 tsp clear honey
½ tsp ground cinnamon
½ tsp freshly grated nutmeg
1 clove
1 tbls lemon juice
1 tsp brandy
50 g (2 oz) dried apricots
410 g (14½ oz) can peach halves,
    drained
25 g (1 oz) sultanas

Place the sugar and water in a large saucepan and heat gently until the sugar has dissolved. Stir in the honey, cinnamon, nutmeg, clove, lemon juice and brandy. Bring to the boil, then reduce the heat.

Add the apricots, cover, and simmer for 15 minutes. Stir in the peaches and simmer for a further 5 minutes until the fruit is tender. Remove the cloves. Stir in the sultanas and serve the fruit salad hot.

Serving idea: Serve with whipped cream and sweet crisp biscuits.
Variations: Use other dried fruit such as prunes, pears or figs instead of the apricots. Rum or apricot brandy may replace the brandy.

49

Atholl brose

25 g (1 oz) fine oatmeal
2 tbls whisky
1 tbls thick honey
142 ml (5 fl oz) carton double cream

Place the oatmeal, whisky and honey in a heavy saucepan and stir well. Set aside for about 15 minutes, then heat gently, stirring constantly, for about 1 minute until the honey has melted and the mixture is thick. Transfer to a bowl and set aside to cool.

Gradually beat the cream into the oatmeal mixture until thick and evenly blended. Spoon into 2 individual glasses and chill in the refrigerator for 1 hour before serving.

Serving idea: Serve with shortbread fingers.

Variation: For a less rich version use plain unsweetened yoghurt instead of cream.

Coffee granita

2 tbls Continental or other strong blend
freshly ground coffee
50 g (2 oz) caster sugar
200 ml (7 fl oz) boiling water

Put the coffee and sugar in a jug and stir in the boiling water. Stir until the coffee and sugar have dissolved, then set aside to cool.

Strain into a rigid container, cover and chill in the refrigerator for at least 30 minutes. Transfer to the freezing compartment of the refrigerator or to the freezer and freeze for at least 2 hours or until completely solid.

Remove from the container and quickly chop into chunks with a heavy, sharp knife. Return to the container and freeze again until required.

Serve straight from the freezer, in glasses.

Serving idea: Serve with whipped cream.

Variation: Stir 1 tsp rum into the cooled coffee liquid.

Lemon mousse

finely grated rind and juice of 1 lemon
15 g (½ oz) sachet powdered gelatine
2 eggs, separated
40 g (1½ oz) caster sugar
a few crystallized lemon slices, to
decorate

Make the lemon juice up to 65 ml (2½ fl oz) with water. Sprinkle the gelatine over the liquid in a small heatproof bowl, then leave for a few minutes until spongy. Stand the bowl in a pan of hot water and stir over a low heat until the gelatine has dissolved. Remove from the heat and allow to cool slightly.

Put the egg yolks in a bowl with the lemon rind and sugar. Stand over a pan of hot water and whisk well until pale and fluffy. Remove the bowl from the water and gradually stir in the cooled liquid gelatine.

Whisk the egg whites stiffly, then fold lightly but thoroughly into the lemon mixture, using a large metal spoon. Pour into 2 individual glasses or dishes and chill in the refrigerator for at least 4 hours until set. Decorate with lemon slices before serving.

Serving idea: Serve with sponge fingers, almond macaroons or walnut meringue biscuits.

Variations: For a richer mousse, fold 5 tbls lightly whipped cream into the mixture before adding the egg whites. Or pipe rosettes of whipped cream round the edge of the mousse. Finely grated orange rind and juice of one orange may be substituted, for an orange mousse. To make a fresh lime mousse, use the rind and juice of 2 limes instead of lemon.

● Top: Coffee granita
Bottom right: Lemon mousse
Bottom left: Atholl brose

Oaty apricot crumble

50 g (2 oz) plain flour
½ tsp ground cinnamon
40 g (1½ oz) margarine or butter, diced
40 g (1½ oz) demerara sugar
25 g (1 oz) rolled oats
350 g (12 oz) fresh apricots, halved and stoned
finely grated rind of ½ orange
25 g (1 oz) sugar

Heat the oven to 190°C, 375°F, Gas Mark 5. Sift the flour with the cinnamon into a mixing bowl. Add the margarine and rub into the mixture until it resembles fine breadcrumbs. Stir in the demerara sugar and oats.

Place the apricots in a 600 ml (1 pint) pie dish. Stir in the orange rind and sugar. Spoon over the crumble topping and bake in the oven for 30-35 minutes until the apricots are tender and the topping is golden brown.

Serving idea: Serve warm with custard or cream.
Variations: Use crushed ginger biscuits instead of the rolled oats. Apples, plums, rhubarb or gooseberries may replace the apricots.

Rhubarb fool

225 g (8 oz) fresh rhubarb, cut into
2·5 cm (1 inch) lengths
40 g (1½ oz) demerara sugar
grated rind of 1 small orange
1 tbls water
100 ml (3½ fl oz) double cream
1 tsp Pernod (optional)

Place the rhubarb, sugar, orange rind and water in a saucepan. Simmer over a very low heat for about 15 minutes until the rhubarb is tender. Drain and set aside to cool.

Beat the cream until thick and stir in the Pernod, if using. Fold into the cooled rhubarb. Divide the mixture between 2 glasses and chill in the refrigerator for at least 1 hour before serving.

Serving idea: Serve with crisp almond-flavoured biscuits.
Variation: Add 1 tsp ground ginger to the rhubarb with the orange rind and omit the Pernod.

Blackcurrant sorbet

175 g (6 oz) fresh or frozen
blackcurrants, topped and tailed
175 ml (6 fl oz) water
50 g (2 oz) caster sugar
1 teaspoon lemon juice
1 egg white

Put the blackcurrants into a saucepan with 3 tablespoons of the water and simmer over a gentle heat until the fruit is pulpy. Rub through a nylon sieve.

Put the sugar and the remaining water in a heavy-based saucepan and gently heat until the sugar has dissolved. Increase the heat and cook rapidly until the syrup reaches 110-112°C, 230-234°F. (If you do not have a sugar thermometer, test by dropping a little of the syrup from a small spoon on to a dish. The syrup should form a fine, thin thread.) Allow to cool completely.

Stir the syrup into the blackcurrant purée with the lemon juice. Pour into a freezer container and, stirring occasionally, freeze for about 1½ hours, until mushy.

Beat the egg white until it forms soft peaks. Fold into the blackcurrant mixture and freeze. Beat once after 1 hour, then cover, seal and freeze again.

Variation: Use redcurrants instead of blackcurrants.

• Left to right: Blackcurrant sorbet; Rhubarb fool; Oaty apricot crumble

• Top: Pears in white wine; bottom right: Iced cucumber soup

Pears in white wine

thinly pared rind and juice of 1 lemon
5 tbls medium white wine
5 tbls water
40 g (1½ oz) caster sugar
2 firm dessert pears, peeled, cored, but
  left whole
1 tsp arrowroot

Place the lemon rind and juice, wine, water and sugar in a saucepan. Bring to the boil, stirring frequently, until the sugar has dissolved.

Place the pears in the pan and poach gently in the syrup for about 30 minutes or until tender, turning carefully from time to time. Remove from the heat and set aside to cool completely.

Remove the pears with a slotted spoon and stand them upright in a serving dish. Mix the arrowroot with a little of the syrup, then pour back into the pan and bring to the boil, stirring until thickened. Cook for a further 2 minutes, stirring. Remove from the heat and set aside to cool, then strain over the pears.

Serving idea: Serve with single cream or ice cream.
Variation: Poach the pears as described then coat in chocolate sauce, made by gently heating together 50 g (2 oz) plain chocolate with 1 tbls water, stirring occasionally, until melted.

54

Iced cucumber soup

½ medium cucumber, peeled
*½ medium Spanish onion, peeled
  and chopped*
300 ml (½ pint) milk
*75 ml (3 fl oz) homemade chicken
  stock*
salt and pepper
20 g (¾ oz) butter
15 g (½ oz) plain flour
*½ teaspoon chopped fresh or a pinch
  of dried mint*
75 ml (3 fl oz) single cream
diced cucumber, drained, to garnish

Chop the cucumber roughly and place it in a saucepan with the onion, milk, stock and salt and pepper to taste, and bring to just under boiling point.

Simmer gently over a low heat for about 30 minutes, until the vegetables are soft. Cool slightly then purée in a liquidizer or food processor or through a fine sieve.

Melt the butter in the rinsed-out pan and stir in the flour. Cook gently for 2-3 minutes, stirring constantly.

Remove the pan from the heat and gradually stir in the cucumber liquid, then add the mint.

Return to the heat and bring gently to the boil, stirring constantly.

Simmer for 5-6 minutes, then pour the soup into a large mixing bowl. Cover with cling film to prevent a skin forming. Cool, then chill for 3 hours.

Whisk the cream into the soup and pour either into 2 individual bowls or into a small tureen. Sprinkle the diced cucumber on top.

Lamb fillet en croûte

2 lamb leg steaks, about 175 g (6 oz)
  each, trimmed
salt and pepper
½ tsp fresh chopped thyme or a pinch
  of dried thyme
1 tbls vegetable oil
15 g (½ oz) margarine or butter
1 shallot, very finely chopped
175 g (6 oz) frozen puff pastry, thawed
beaten egg
watercress sprigs, to garnish
For the sauce
25 g (1 oz) margarine or butter
50 g (2 oz) mushrooms, chopped
20 g (¾ oz) plain flour
300 ml (½ pint) chicken stock
pinch of ground mace

Place one lamb steak on top of the other. Tie like a parcel with fine string, season lightly with salt and pepper and sprinkle with the thyme.

Heat the oil in a frying pan, add the lamb and fry over a gentle heat for about 5 minutes, turning once, to brown on both sides. Remove from the pan and set aside to cool.

Melt the margarine in the pan, add the shallot and fry gently for 2-3 minutes until softened. Remove from the heat and allow to cool.

Heat the oven to 220°C, 425°F, Gas Mark 7. Roll out the pastry thinly on a lightly floured work surface, reserving the trimmings. Remove the string from the lamb, place in the centre of the pastry and spoon over the shallot. Wrap the lamb in the pastry to enclose it completely, dampening the edges and pressing them well together to seal.

Place on a dampened baking sheet, seam side down. Re-roll the pastry trimmings and cut out leaves. Use to decorate the surface of the pastry. Brush all over with beaten egg.

Bake in the oven for 15 minutes. Reduce the heat to 180°C, 350°F, Gas Mark 4 and bake for a further 20 minutes until the pastry is golden brown.

Just before the lamb is ready, make the sauce. Melt the margarine in a small saucepan, add the mushrooms and fry gently for 2-3 minutes until softened. Stir in the flour and cook for 1 minute. Gradually stir in the stock and bring to the boil. Simmer for 2-3 minutes, then season to taste and stir in the mace.

Transfer the lamb en croûte to a heated serving dish, garnish with watercress sprigs and serve cut into slices. Hand the sauce separately in a jug or sauceboat.

Variation: For pork en croûte use 225 g (8 oz) pork fillet and wrap in rashers of streaky bacon before frying.

French beans in tomato sauce

1 ½ tbls olive oil
1 garlic clove, crushed
1 large tomato, skinned and
  chopped
300 g (10 oz) French beans, halved
salt and pepper

Heat the oil in a heavy-based saucepan, add the garlic and fry gently for 1-2 minutes until softened. Stir in the tomato, then add the beans. Add enough water to just cover the beans, season to taste and bring to the boil.

Reduce the heat, cover and simmer for 20-25 minutes until the beans are tender. Towards the end of cooking time remove the lid and increase the heat to reduce and thicken the sauce.

Chicory and citrus salad

½ pink grapefruit, peeled and
  segmented
1 small avocado peeled and thinly
  sliced
1 tbls olive oil
2 tsp cider vinegar
pinch of sugar
salt and pepper
1 head chicory leaves, separated
watercress sprigs to garnish

Drain the juices from the grapefruit segments into a small bowl. Add the avocado slices and toss well. Arrange a row of avocado slices along the centre of 2 individual serving dishes.

In the same bowl beat together with a fork the oil, vinegar, sugar and salt and pepper.

Arrange the grapefruit segments and chicory leaves around the avocado. Pour the dressing over the salad and garnish with watercress.

Serving idea: This salad also makes a good accompaniment to a light, baked fish such as trout or sole.

● Lamb fillet en croûte; French beans in tomato sauce

• Peach melba

Peach Melba

3 tbls sugar
300 ml (½ pint) water
a few drops of lemon juice
*2 ripe, firm peaches, skinned, halved
   and stoned*
2 scoops vanilla ice cream
*75 ml (3 fl oz) whipping cream,
   whipped to decorate*
For the sauce
100 g (4 oz) fresh raspberries
1½ tbls icing sugar, sifted

Place the sugar, water and lemon juice in a saucepan and heat gently, stirring, until the sugar has dissolved. Bring to the boil, then reduce the heat, add the peaches and poach gently for 10 minutes or until tender. Remove from the heat and set aside to cool in the syrup.

To make the sauce, rub the raspberries through a sieve into a bowl. Gradually beat the icing sugar into the raspberry purée.

To serve, place a scoop of ice cream in 2 individual glass dishes. Top each portion of ice cream with 2 peach halves, coat each with half the Melba sauce and top with whipped cream.

Variation: Omit the cream and sprinkle with a few toasted flaked almonds or chopped hazelnuts.

MENU

Melon, walnut and avocado salad

Baked poussins with herbs

Courgettes with lime

Chocolate mousse

•

Macon Blanc or Chablis

Melon, walnut and avocado salad

¼ small honeydew melon, seeded
1 small avocado pear
8 lettuce leaves, shredded
15 g (½ oz) chopped walnuts
1 tsp sultanas
For the dressing
2 tbls olive oil
2 tsp red wine vinegar
1 tsp lemon juice
¼ tsp French mustard
pinch of sugar
pinch of dried dill
salt and pepper

Scoop out the melon flesh with a melon baller or cut into 1 cm (½ inch) cubes. Place in a bowl.

Halve the avocado, discard the stone, and peel. Cut the flesh into 1 cm (½ inch) cubes, add to the melon balls and toss together.

Arrange the lettuce in a shallow salad bowl, then spoon over the melon and avocado. Sprinkle with the walnuts and sultanas.

To make the dressing, place all the ingredients in a screw-top jar and shake vigorously until well blended. Adjust the seasoning to taste, then pour over the salad and serve immediately.

Variation: Instead of the walnuts and sultanas use 1 celery stalk, chopped, and a few seeded grapes.

• Melon, walnut and avocado salad

Baked poussins with herbs

2 poussins
1 lemon, halved
25 g (1 oz) butter, softened
salt and pepper
1 tsp chopped fresh tarragon or ½ tsp
    dried tarragon
fresh tarragon sprigs, to garnish

Heat the oven to 180°C, 350°F, Gas Mark 4. Cut 2 pieces of foil each large enough to contain a poussin, and place a poussin, breast side up, on each piece of foil.

Squeeze one lemon half over the poussins. Cut the remaining half into slices and place in the body cavity of each poussin.

Spread the butter over the poussins, season with salt and pepper and sprinkle with tarragon. Wrap each bird firmly in the foil.

Roast the poussins in the oven for 25 minutes. Open the foil and turn the poussins over. Cook for a further 5 minutes, then turn the poussins back breast side up, and with the foil still open cook for a further 10 minutes to brown them.

Transfer the poussins to a heated serving dish and pour the cooking juices over them. Garnish with fresh tarragon and serve immediately.

Serving idea: Serve with new potatoes and French beans as an alternative to courgettes.

Variation: The poussins can also be served cold, when the tarragon-flavoured juices turn to jelly. Vary the flavour by using different herbs – try a mixture of chopped parsley and marjoram.

Courgettes with lime

15g (½oz) margarine or butter
1 tbls olive oil
½ onion, thinly sliced
1 garlic clove, crushed
225g (8oz) courgettes, sliced
1 tbls fresh lime juice
salt and pepper

Melt the margarine with the oil in a frying pan. Add the onion and garlic and fry gently for 5 minutes.

Add the courgettes, increase the heat and fry briskly for 10 minutes, shaking the pan constantly and turning the courgettes from time to time. Stir in the lime juice, season to taste and serve.

Variation: Use lemon for lime juice.

Chocolate mousse

100g (4oz) plain chocolate
2 eggs, separated
2 tsp rum
15g (½oz) butter
75ml (3fl oz) whipping cream,
  whipped to decorate

Place the chocolate in a heatproof bowl over a saucepan of hot water and heat gently until melted. Remove from the heat. Remove the bowl from the pan and stir in the egg yolks, one at a time, followed by the rum and the butter.

Whisk the egg whites stiffly, then fold lightly into the chocolate mixture.

Spoon the mousse into 2 glass dishes and chill for 2-3 hours or until set. Serve decorated with whipped cream.

• Courgettes with lime; Baked poussins with herbs; Chocolate mousse

Caesar salad

1 tbls vegetable oil
2 small white bread slices, crusts
  removed, cut into dice
1 small crisp lettuce, shredded
2 tbls grated Parmesan cheese
For the dressing
1 egg yolk, beaten
3 tbls olive oil
1 tbls white wine vinegar
1 tsp lemon juice
1 garlic clove, crushed

Combine all the ingredients for the dressing in a screw-top jar. Shake well together and set aside for 1 hour.

Heat the oil in a frying pan. Add the diced bread and fry for 3-4 minutes, turning constantly, until crisp and lightly browned. Remove from the heat. Drain the croûtons on absorbent paper and leave to cool.

Place the lettuce in a salad bowl. Pour the dressing over the lettuce and toss well. Sprinkle the cheese over the salad and top with the croûtons. Serve the salad at once.

Variations: Fry 1 rasher streaky bacon, rinded and chopped, with the croûtons. Two anchovy fillets, soaked in milk for 20 minutes, then drained and finely chopped, may be added to the dressing.

Celebration steak

2 rump steaks, each weighing 175 g
  (6 oz)
½ tbls vegetable oil
1 orange, sliced, to garnish
For the marinade
5 tbls orange juice
½ small onion, chopped
1 tbls ground coriander
½ tbls olive oil
1 large garlic clove, crushed

Mix together all the marinade ingredients in a large bowl. Add the steaks and turn to coat in the marinade. Cover and leave in a cool place for 1-2 hours.

Remove the steak, reserving the marinade, and drain on absorbent kitchen paper. Heat the oil in a frying pan, add the steaks and cook over a high heat, turning once, for 6-10 minutes, until the steaks are done to your

liking. Transfer the steaks to a heated serving dish and keep warm.

Place the reserved marinade in a blender goblet and liquidize, then pour into a saucepan and heat gently for 5-10 minutes, until syrupy, adding a little water if necessary.

Serve the steak garnished with orange slices and hand the sauce separately in a jug or sauceboat.

Serving ideas: Serve with French fries or jacket potatoes with soured cream and chives.
Variation: Use pork chops instead of the steak, increasing the cooking time to about 15 minutes.

● Celebration steak; Caesar salad; Exotic fruit fool

Exotic fruit fool

1 egg yolk
25 g (1 oz) caster sugar
1 tsp custard powder
150 ml (¼ pint) milk
1 large ripe mango, skinned
142 ml (5 fl oz) carton double cream, lightly whipped
grated chocolate, to decorate

Beat the egg yolk, sugar and custard powder in a bowl with a little of the milk to make a smooth paste. Heat the remaining milk to just below boiling point, then stir into the egg mixture. Return to the saucepan and heat very gently, stirring, until the custard thickens. Do not allow to boil. Remove from the heat and set aside to cool completely.

Place the mango flesh in a blender goblet and process until smooth. Mix the mango purée with the cold custard. Fold in the cream and pour into a serving dish.

Chill in the refrigerator for at least 1 hour. Sprinkle with a little grated chocolate before serving.

Serving idea: Serve with sponge fingers or crisp sweet biscuits.
Variation: Instead of fresh mango use a 425 g (15 oz) can sliced mango, drained.

INDEX

*Note:*this index includes variations suggested in recipes as well as the main recipes